T0195067

DISCOVERING
WHO I AM
(AFTER THE STORM)

SHONDOLYN LATHAM

authorHOUSE®

AuthorHouse™
1663 Liberty Drive
Bloomington, IN 47403
www.authorhouse.com
Phone: 833-262-8899

Published by AuthorHouse 01/18/2021

ISBN: 978-1-6655-1421-7 (sc)
ISBN: 978-1-6655-1422-4 (hc)
ISBN: 978-1-6655-1431-6 (e)

Library of Congress Control Number: 2021901265

Contents

Discovering Who I Am after the Storm

would like to start off by saying thank you to all my readers. Thank you for trusting me, supporting me, and wanting to know my story. I didn't have much writing experience, but you read it anyway. For that I am thankful. I am elated that you are here again! Welcome to the better version of me! I'm happy, I'm in tune with myself, and I am free to love, free to give, and free to explore. Most of all, I'm free to live. I've taken off all the boundaries that have had me in bondage for years: fear, grudges, hurt, poverty, etc. Whatever and wherever God is taking me, I'm ready to go!

I have been taking a lot of time to myself lately. I'm working on me. I've been introducing myself to different ways to reidentify myself with myself! I know that sentence seems confusing, but reread it until it makes sense. I've been redirecting my life by finishing up some things that I have been pursuing for a long time. Although I have a clearer view, sometimes it seems as if I'm not getting anywhere. There are so many things that try to clutter my space at times. I'm thankful that I can identify those things before they have a chance to consume me. As I dissect each obstacle, I begin to realize that whatever I speak upon myself is what I manifest. Whatever environment I allow myself to be in, that's the environment or the spirit that I will eventually pick up. I'm not saying that these things changed who I am, but they definitely slowed down my process of manifestation.

Whether it's a job that is not your passion or a person who is not your person, we live and we learn.

Sometimes life brings situations upon us that we can't get away from. The only exception to that type of change is a child or a parent! I love my family dearly, but sometimes if things aren't aligned with your purpose or with what you are trying to manifest, you have to separate yourself from that. Sometimes the separation is from everything that you know to be normal. Normal is not always good, because we get comfortable in normal. Normal makes us settle. Who wouldn't want to settle for comfort? Comfortable feels good if you have no goals and ambitions. I'm an ambitious person. I'm constantly trying to figure out ways to be a better person or just make sure I'm true to me at all times. There is no time for comfort. I want all that God has for me, and I want it in abundance. Being comfortable doesn't allow you to grow or should I say live in your purpose. This year alone I have been put in so many uncomfortable situations, so my takeaway from all the discomfort or the message that I'm getting is loud and clear. Get up, manifest (start speaking) some things into my life, live in my purpose, and give my dreams life! I'm stepping out on faith. I will get to my destination. I have to get uncomfortable and put in the work. James 2:26 states, "For as the body without the spirit is dead, so faith without works is dead." Getting comfortable in your situation is not an option. Get uncomfortable so you can power through whatever it is. Never mind the outcome; it won't be what we want sometimes. The outcome doesn't always work in our favor, but the experience can always teach us a lesson.

Sometimes when we go through things, we think that just because we don't have that issue anymore that we are okay now. That is not always the case. For the past year, I have been thinking that since my load has been lifted, I was going to all of a sudden be free. I've had to go through a process. My body was in fight or flight mode for twenty-four years! I didn't know that until I didn't have that one thing to fight for anymore. Ironically, while going through the process, I had to readjust my direction of energy on myself. I had to learn to be selfish so that I could give me what I needed. As my daughter always says about herself, "I don't play about me!" She gave me some great food for thought. I've had to speak and manifest some positive affirmations into my life. I am so thankful that I am seeing those things come to pass. I had no idea that God was going to lead me down this path. I'm glad He did, because I've never been more at peace than I am now!

I am a small-town girl with big dreams that have been with me since I was a child. As a child, dreams are just that: dreams. We have no clue that those dreams are most of our realities. We don't realize it until we become adults. The way those realities are recognized is that they follow us or show up in our thoughts throughout our lives. I truly believe that we all are shown our purposes on earth in our imaginations as children, but as children, we can't bring those dreams to life, and they remain right where they are in our imaginations. There have been many cases where people can and do bring their childhood imagination to life. As an adult, you begin to understand, and wisdom has time to kick in. Steve Harvey talks about himself as a child telling his dad that he wanted to be on TV. He didn't know how it was going to happen, but he knew one day that it would happen. He had faith! Again, faith without works is dead (James 2:26)! Now he's living his dream.

As we grow older and start to go through the process of life, we begin to get a clearer picture of those childhood dreams. Some of us realize that we still have a desire for what we saw in our imaginations, and we make them our realities. I love to write. Now I'm a second-time author, all because I loved homework when I was in school (or because I had something to write about). Unfortunately, as we begin to live, life sometimes causes us to step off the path of our dreams. Like many of us, I got off my path. I needed to gain life's wisdom in order to walk back onto that path or should I say walk back into my purpose. Better yet, "live in my destiny," or even better, "Give my dreams life!" My life was aligned perfectly to bring me to my purpose.

Life has educated me in a way that no university can, and my life has given me an amazing story. We all have a story. My story has allowed me to grow so much in my mind, body, and soul. I thank God for my experiences. Each experience has taught me some valuable lessons, good and bad. The most valuable lessons that I have learned are invest in yourself, love yourself, and never put all of your eggs in one basket. Never give up on yourself. Love unconditionally. Do unto others as you would have them do unto you. You will be rewarded with riches in glory. Sometimes it hurts emotionally when you have been kind to someone who has bad intentions for you. The satisfaction of knowing you did the right thing eventually helps the healing process.

Life takes us all on a journey of the unknown, but as you navigate through it, remember to trust the process. Make sure that you don't dwell too long in the past, and don't think too far into the future. Some of us live so hard for the future that we never give ourselves a chance to live for now. I think that everyone needs to listen to or read the book *The Power of Now* by the profound spiritual teacher Eckhart Tolle. He teaches that sometimes our minds are too loud. We have to learn how to declutter our thoughts and focus on the things that are right in front of us at that moment. Through his experiences, he mastered the ability to teach people how to transform from within. I'm going through that process right now.

I am trying to learn to live in the moment. I find myself having a lot of plans, but sometimes they get stagnant, because I'm trying to complete them all at once. I have been spending a lot of time with myself for the past few months. The revelation from this process is that God has secluded me from all distractions. I am living in a secluded place so that I can get to my goals. I must say it has been very rewarding. I have grown accustomed to my quiet time. I realize I needed it for my sanity. I'm so grateful! God is blessing me!

Some of you who read my first book know a portion of my story. I revealed a lot of struggles within myself that many of you didn't know. That was a very vulnerable time in my life. Vulnerability has advantages and disadvantages. The advantage of being vulnerable is that it allows you to be the purest form of yourself. You offer more of yourself than you should at the weakest point of your life. If you can't manage that part of being vulnerable, it can quickly turn into a disadvantage. Another disadvantage is that when you are in that vulnerable state of mind, it opens you up to trust some people that you shouldn't. Like some say, every lesson is a blessing no matter if it seems like you learned the hard way. I definitely find inspiration in that old saying "what's meant to break you is the very thing that makes you." There are so many old sayings that I grew up listening to my elders quote. Back then, they didn't seem to be meaningful, but as I grew older and life started to really happen, I started quoting them myself. That's when I began to see the significance.

In my first book, I let my heart guide my words to lift some of the pressure that life had put on me. I was vulnerable. In reality, no matter what my state of mind was, I was proud of myself. I accomplished something that many people want to do but don't have the courage to do. I authored a book!

If you don't get anything else from my book, take this

lesson with you: Don't be ashamed to be who you are. Be true to yourself! I want you to know that it's okay to be you, but make sure you represent yourself with the respect and diligence that you give anyone else. It's okay to be honest. It's okay to say no. It's okay to say yes. Make sure that both no and yes make you feel comfortable when you say them. Don't ever use those words to please anyone else if you're not pleased. I will always stay true to who I am. I love me more than anything.

I want to encourage you to keep pushing yourself into your full potential. I encourage you to fight for your dreams. Write that book, take those workout classes, pick up that sketch book, and further your education. Conquer those dreams, and along the way, uplift yourself when others won't. Reading this now is God giving you the green light to chase your dreams. Many of us may think that it's impossible to dream our dreams into reality. I've learned that I can do all things through Christ who strengthens me (Philippians 4:13)! No more self- doubt, and no more feeling sorry for myself. It's time to walk in my purpose. I encourage you to do the same. Again, I can do all things through Christ who strengthens me.

I'm not the type of person to put on a show for the public, but I want to be publicly recognized for my triumphs, my strength to fight, and my will to want more. I want to encourage everyone not to settle for just enough. I don't want to live with just enough. I want more than enough so that I can help others who need help. I have settled for just enough for years. I had no choice. My children needed me. Sometimes that's the price that we pay when we become parents before we get ourselves established in our finances. We never look at the possibility of things going differently than what's expected.

Now that my ill son has transitioned to heaven and my other two children are grown, my life is just beginning.

I consider myself a late bloomer; now I can live for me. I'm thankful because I have a whole lot of wisdom and knowledge to know exactly what I want and what I deserve now! I'm not settling for less. I'm grateful! I want to have all that I need so that I can bless others. I am so thankful for the opportunity to put myself out there to encourage others who are trying to get through tough times in their lives, while I continue *discovering who I am*—this time after the storm!

I'm not outspoken, but I will speak out on situations and circumstances that affect me and the people I love. I love that characteristic about myself. I wasn't always like that. I went through a lot of things that I didn't deserve to go through. To this day and this very moment, I'm still going through some things, but I have been delivered from so many other things. Life is a process, and to go through it, you have to live in it. I encourage you to come up with new ways to make this day better than yesterday.

Just keep pushing. Pick yourself up, and dust yourself off! God won't put more on you than you can bear! *This too shall pass!*

I'm not that person anymore who easily folds and feel sorry for herself when troubles come. I figure out strategies to overcome the beating that those things place on my heart. In other words, I *love me harder!* I do the things I love that don't cost a cent such as long, hot baths and long walks. I read and engage in activities that are going to better me in the long run.

After reading this book, you won't be the same. After reflecting on things of the past (I don't dwell there long), I realize that all the things in my future are for my good and are better than what's been. I can say that I have gained so much strength during this phase of my life. I am not the same! The level of growth that I have achieved in my mind, body, and soul has me more excited to face each day.

I'm confident that all of you who read my first book will enjoy seeing my improvements and growth in this book.

My first book was written strictly off of hurt! I know now that there was a purpose for that publication. That purpose was to show myself and others that after that storm, there is sunshine. I can't say this enough: God won't put more on you than you can bear. Luke 12:12 states, "He continued this subject with His disciples. 'Don't fuss about what's on the table at mealtimes or if the clothes in your closet are in fashion. There is far more to your inner life than the food you put in your stomach, more to your outer appearance than the clothes you hang on your body.

II Corinthians 9:8 says, "God can pour on the blessings in astonishing ways so that you are ready for anything and everything."

No one can receive your blessings but you. What's for

you is for you! Get ready to receive all that is for you, but it's not just going to fall in your lap. You have to work for it. Align your life to manifest your dreams! Anything or any person who is in your life and causing you to operate outside of who you are—get rid of it! You cannot advance if your inner self doesn't feel like you. We all have goals and ambitions. Sometimes along the way, life causes us to lose those dreams. To be honest, if you look back, you had those dreams early in life just like I did. Go back and pick them up. Every human being has a purpose. The uniqueness of it all is that every human being has a different purpose. Find yours, and grow with it! It doesn't matter where you are in your life. Growth comes at all ages and at any given time in your life. I'm overflowing with thanksgiving!

I found my purpose. It took caring for my son, Devin, my whole young adult life until he took his last breath twenty-four years and eleven months after his birth. That journey with Devin made me strong and encouraged me to fight for myself and my happiness. I loved and cared for that little boy harder than anything, and that time molded me into the courageous woman I am today! I will forever be grateful for the journey. My baby boy, I will love you forever. I want you back so badly! Continue to rest in peace, my angel!

I miss you, Devin. You gave Mommy a vision to tell our story. In remembrance of you, I will continue to be a person who helps others through my story.

There will be many more books to come. With each publication, I believe my readers will be inspired watching me grow in my writing and reading my story. I hope that my stories will encourage everyone to pursue their passions and dreams without waiting for that perfect moment. Wherever you are right now is your perfect moment. Whatever your heart desires and makes you happy, go for it. If you know you would do it for free, you have discovered your passion and your purpose. People, please realize that you don't have to be perfect to walk in your purpose. I'm doing something I love, and the title still rings true: I'm *discovering who I am* but this time after the storm!

My heart is fully engaged in this. Through this process, I have discovered that writing is a job that doesn't feel like a job. We all want to experience, at some point in our lives, work that doesn't feel like work. It feels good just to type that. When you are doing something that doesn't feel like work and are anxious to do it daily, you have discovered your purpose. Live in it! Make the best of it! Do it to the absolute best of your ability! After all, it's your signature! That will be how people identify you.

I had to create an office space with furniture, printers, the whole nine yards. I completed my personal training certification! I have a website that showcases my products and services. I'm proud of myself. I get to be happy. After all, I deserve it.

I got a lot of positive and negative feedback from my first book. I'm grateful for that. Critics are essential to growth. Through the criticism, we realize that any endeavor we embark upon is like starting a new job. We have to learn the process. When you start a new job, you're not going to go right in and master it. It takes time.

Since the release of my first book, I have been feeling at peace. August 25, 2019— I remember the day clearly. That day was the first time I felt happy since Devin passed away. *Happy* is a beautiful word that can have several meanings. At this moment, it means that I'm feeling extremely peaceful sitting here on my couch, listening to music. I have had the same song on replay for the past hour: "My Song" by H.E.R. The lyrics that stand out to me are "Let me sing my song. I know that when I listen. I find what I been missing right here in my heart." As I sit here and listen to me—my thoughts, my heart, and my body—I realize that I'm not where I want to be, but in this phase of my life, I'm definitely where I need to be. After losing Devin, life has allowed me to start to focus on what I want, what I need, and what goals I will accomplish.

God reveals so many things to us on our daily walks through life, but He leaves it up to us to grasp the concept and true meanings of those revelations. As long as I'd been thinking about writing, it wasn't until I started doing it that I realized how therapeutic it was and still is for me.

I contemplated changing the name of this book and was overthinking it, but as soon as I started writing, I felt it was appropriate to keep the title, because I'm still discovering me.

Being so young when I became a mother and then ending up having a kid who was ill his whole life caused me to put my life on hold. It threw me behind on a lot of milestones I should have reached by now, but it's okay. I was set apart to go through that process. I'm grateful.

Since I am a late bloomer in pursuit of her dreams, I focus on a lot of topics, goals, and accomplishments this time around. Happiness is one topic, and it could well be the most important one. The meaning of the word *happy* that shows up on Google is a range of positive emotions: joy, pride, contentment, gratitude, pleasure, and satisfaction.

In Sonja Lyubomirsky's 2007 book, *The How of Happiness,* the positive psychology researcher describes happiness as "the experience of joy, contentment, or positive well-being combined with a sense that one's life is good, meaningful and worthwhile." I agree with that definition wholeheartedly. To add to it, my peace of mind is my happiness as well.

As I sit here listening to this song by H.E.R., I hear it from a different perspective. I'm not counting on anyone to make me happy. I have to obtain my own happiness. I can search for happiness from many sources, but if I can't find it within myself, I'm wasting my time searching.

These days, I'm on a mission each day: getting my thoughts together, setting goals for myself, and achieving them one by one. I'm happy to just have a list of goals to work on for the betterment of myself. As I cross each goal off my list, enduring the process of each one, I am successful in giving my dreams life.

There will never be anything that will fill that void that I have since Devin transitioned to heaven, but the inspiration and joy that he brought to our lives gives us the memory of his contagiously awesome personality. I find myself stopping in my tracks when I think I smell him. Even when I walk by a mirror, my own image makes me take a second look, because I see him in me. I try to fight back my tears when the thought of him weighs so heavily on my mind. I realize that fighting those tears is impossible! I experienced a loss that is a parent's worst nightmare. When I get too caught up in the grief, I start to think about his bubbly personality and how he never wanted to see me sad or hurting. That's why I feel that my next publication will be strictly about him and his walk in life. He was the sweetest, kindest, most lovable, humble, and selfless human being I knew. I can count the times that I saw him angry on one hand, and I was in his presence every single day for almost twenty-five years.

I don't want this book to be sad, but again I say, I want you to feel my heart just as you did in my first book. I ask that you remember that I am a grieving mother. There will be parts that are sad, but that's okay.

I have been picking up the pieces of my life day by day. My mental and physical body has a lot to recover from. I'm so proud of myself for being able to endure the longevity of my experience as Devin's mom. He made the experience soooo much easier for me. He taught me how to love unconditionally, endure, and be courageous. He taught me how to be strong and power through the impossible. He taught me how to speak up. He literally walked me through many experiences. We were hand in hand everywhere we went. He was so confident in me while I protected and cared for him. For example, when he left home for school, he had to use a mobility cane to guide him as he walked, because he couldn't see. When he got home or when we went places on the weekends, he didn't think about that mobility cane. He automatically knew that I was going to protect him.

In the twenty-four years and eleven months that Devin was on this earth, I was amazed at the bond we shared. We were joined at the hip. I miss his touch. I miss his voice. I miss his laugh. I miss his kind spirit, but I'm thankful for the memories.

I couldn't move for him being up under me. I loved every minute of it. He slept in my bed his whole life. Even when I tried to encourage him to sleep in his own room, he would end up back in my room within two days, toys and all.

I didn't mind, and I see now that it had a purpose for that close bond. He didn't have long to be with me.

Devin taught me how to see without my eyes. When I tell you that's the best experience ever, believe it. He made me realize that my hands were soft! That's another thing that was amazing to me. I didn't realize that my hands were soft. He had to tell me. He would rub my hands and arms to see how many scratches I had gotten from work. He didn't like the fact that I was doing a job that was scratching me up, and that made me start applying lotion to my hands after every wash. He could get a visual of my hands only through touch. As any mom would, I wanted him to have the smoothest visual ever. Even though I took care of him, he took care of me in his own way. He was so caring. He would rub my feet if I had a long day at work, but that didn't last long, because I would tell him, "No, let me rub your feet. You deserve it for being so sweet." Even when playing with his little sister, he let her have her way. She made all of the game rules. He was just present, playing what she wanted to play until he couldn't take anymore. Even then, he wasn't rude when he dismissed himself. He just got up and left in the middle of the game or of her reading him a story.

He drew the line when she called him "little big brother." He wasn't big on speaking out, but something about her calling him that struck a nerve. He told her that he didn't care if she was getting taller than him. He was still the big brother.

Devin found joy in being the middle kid—the "knee baby," as they call it. He said he got the opportunity to be the little and the big brother. Leave it to Devin to find joy in being the middle child. It didn't surprise me that he found joy in that. Devin taught us how to find joy in any situation.

I thank God for all three of my children. They are great kids. All three of them have big hearts, and they love hard. I pray that my two kids who remain here on earth are protected from joy-stealing people. I pray that they reach their full potential and discover their purpose. I didn't experience the terrible loss alone when

Devin transitioned to heaven; they did too. My oldest son sometimes walks around the house getting things that belonged to Devin, trying get a whiff of his scent. It hurts me to see them long for their brother. They are so young to have experienced this loss. God, please be with us!

So far in this process of discovering myself, I've been enjoying strengthening relationships. I have been amazed at some of the relationships I lost that took years to build. I'm not sure how or why those relationships ended so abruptly, but seasons change.

I don't want to use a lot of positive energy focusing on the negative. I just have to believe that it's a part of the process and move on. I have discovered that being closed off to people was why a few of my relationships not prospering. Now that I'm older and wiser, I know the importance of building relationships. I believe that is another lesson that I learned while being Devin's mom. We had an amazing mother-son relationship.

Here I am at 2:55 a.m. on a Saturday morning, and I can't sleep. I decide to check *The New York Times* best sellers list: that's where I want to be, and in order to have what you desire, you have to surround yourself with people who have made it to where you are trying to go. After reading the list, I can choose a book. Thousands of books come up on the audible website as I browse for an inspirational book to listen to. I choose *Girl, Stop Apologizing* by Rachel Hollis. I'm one hour and forty-four minutes into this eight-hour-long book, and she has already inspired me. She has given me confirmation that I am doing the right thing by pursuing my what ifs and my dreams. What if I finish all the things I started but couldn't finish because Devin became ill? It's so coincidental that I chose this book. It's confirmation that I need to keep going. My direction is clear. The foundation has been set. Go for it! As the late Overseer Glenn Jefferson would say,

"It's not how you start, it's how you finish. Finish strong!"

That is what I intend to do.

Lately, I have been asking myself not only *what if* but *why*.

Why

I 've learned that there has to be a "why" to everything you do. Before you engage in something, you have to have already contemplated why you are going to do it. Every action has a consequence. My why has pushed me to crave success. My why has given me a vision of not wanting to live from paycheck to paycheck. My why has given me the ability to see the bigger picture. I have been inspired by recent events in my life to never stop pushing for better. I don't think that my vision has ever been clearer than it is now. When I look back, I believe that I've always had the vision. I just wasn't focused. I was vested in taking care of my ill son. At that time, my vision and focus were solely on him. On May 20, 2019, we lost the battle. I watched my son look at me for the last time with those big, beautiful eyes before he took his last breath! Today, on May 21, 2020, one year and one day since he transitioned, I still miss him terribly. Today I stood and watched as Jewel Monument placed the headstone on his grave. The numbness is still there, but I made it a year without him. Going through all that I went through with him has given me a desire to help people more than ever.

I have always been a quiet and soft-spoken person. I still remain in disbelief that I want to speak to the world no matter how many are in the audience. I want to spread positivity in abundance. I love who I am and the calling that has been placed upon my life. I have goals and ambitions to keep fighting for what I want, just as I did for my son. I'm so thankful for the opportunity to have been his mother, and most importantly, I find comfort in knowing that God allowed me to be there for his first and last breaths. As hard as it was to watch, the strength that I gained from God through Devin allowed me to endure that.

Lately I have been trying to put a time frame on the things that I want to accomplish. As human beings, that's natural. To the best of our abilities, we do what we need to do to keep on track. I went out at the beginning on 2020, bought a planner, and proclaimed that I was going to write in it weekly to keep on track for achieving my goals, no matter how big or small they were. It started out good, but as the weeks went on, I got off track. That's okay. Life was still happening. As long as you get back on track, that's all that matters. The one thing that I did keep focus on was my commitment to myself. I kept my finances on track as best I could. I also made it my goal to take better care of myself. I chose things that impacted my mood positively so that I could not sweat the small stuff. I vowed to start my day the best possible way. When I open my eyes, I give thanks for being alive and in my right mind. I immediately drink a sixteen-ounce bottle of water to wake up my digestive system.

I made a pact with myself to indulge in weekly detox baths and stay on top of becoming financially stable. I have the desire to work for myself, so I have to always invest in myself. Pulling myself out of that manufacturing plant is my ultimate goal. I'm still in that phase, but I will accomplish it. "Ask, and it shall be given you. Seek, and ye shall find. Knock, and it shall be opened unto you" (Matthew 7:7).

I'm too talented to be confined for eight hours at someone else's job. Don't get me wrong. That job has provided for me and my children, but I want more than just a paycheck. I want peace and gratification. I want to help people be the best versions of themselves while helping myself be the best version of me. I don't want to be dependent upon a job that could close the doors at any time, leaving me to try to figure out what's next.

Once I asked myself why, I decided to redirect the message of this book as revelation for myself. Realizing that focusing on me isn't being selfish, I'm dedicating my book to myself and all others who ask themselves why. Everyone's why will not be the same. The difference between each why is impacted by what we go through in our everyday lives.

Why do you love yourself? Why do you want to succeed so bad? Why do you want to help others when you have been torn down by people so badly this past year? Why do you want to get out of bed every morning? Why have you stayed at the same job for the last twenty years? Why are you writing another book? Why do you want to manage a cooperation? As quiet as you once were, why do you want to speak in front of a crowd? What changes happened within you to make you want to do it? Why? These are my whys. I encourage you to find your why.

There are several explanations to my whys, and you will read about them in this book. Thank you for purchasing it, and thank you for reading. To all who support me in whatever I do, I especially want to thank you! Amazingly there are some of you who do! I must repeat: I am so grateful. You may see that sentence several times—I am grateful!

Now to explain some of my whys.

Why do I love myself?

love myself because I'm worth it. Look at me. I'm beautiful and strong. I love every part of me, flaws and all. If I can't love me, how can I love others? I love that I have become this last year. I love me for my strength to endure. My will to live. My determination to want more. My drive to not settle for less than I deserve. Like the lessons you learn in school, life throws critical thinking lessons at you with a different analogy. The only difference is that in life, you don't have anyone to tell you if you're right or wrong. Down the road, you have to reuse those skills you learned in the past. We think that the classes they give us in school are not relevant to our future. To tell the truth, life happens so fast after school that you will have solved a school-related problem without realizing it.

Devin was my joy. He hugged me daily, and he was the spitting image of me. I didn't see the potential in myself, but ironically, I saw me in him: my potential, my gentleness, my humbleness. He mirrored the image of me.

I see him so strong in me. He taught me an unconditional love that is rare. He was my pride and joy! All of my children are. DJaye and Kadence stand behind me ten toes down if I need protection. I laugh at them, because that's exactly what I will do for them.

I wake up every day and put my clothes on just like everyone else, but I portray something in my soul that a lot of people don't have: unconditional love for myself. I knew how I wanted to be loved at a young age. I always seemed to be searching for it. That was a big mistake. After a few times of bumping my head, I got it. One thing I can say is when I knew love wasn't there, I had no problem dismissing myself.

I have drive and motivation to be successful. My definition of success is not having to struggle anymore, not having to depend on someone else to take care of me, and most importantly, learning to stand on my own two feet no matter what my circumstances are. The ultimate success is being happy with yourself before you can be happy with someone else. I'm ready!

I mentioned in my first book having the feeling of never being able to complete tasks that I start. I discovered that was because I had to finish the task of being a phenomenal mom and support system to Devin. Through all the trials, tribulations, and completion of the ultimate task, I still have that thirst for success. Now that I've endured, I realize that it's my time to love me enough to give my dreams life!

Why do I want to succeed so bad?

I want better for myself. I'm tired of working a nine-to-five job that doesn't care if I live or die. I'm tired of barely getting by. I'm tired of living paycheck to paycheck. I want to empower people. I want to show people that you don't have to be confined to your circumstances. A little bit of fight will help you at least get started on making your life better. It's not easy. People are not going to receive you with open arms. Life in general will throw curve balls along the way. You have to fight for that spot that is rightfully yours. I'm grateful! God put a fire inside of me that didn't go out when Devin transitioned to heaven. I still have goals, dreams, and ambitions, and I will fulfill them all. As I continue to come up with ideas to become the best version of myself, I'm stepping out on faith to do all things through Christ who strengthens me. I'm tired of being in a place where you don't get recognized for your skills. I'm not using my skills anymore to make the rich richer. I'm going to sow into myself and my family.

Why do you want to help others when you have been torn down so badly this past year?

E very individual isn't bad, and every individual doesn't have the motive to suck the life out of you. It takes a while to weed out the bad, but along the way, you learn who's genuine and who's not. I love being happy. I can't and won't let anybody take that from me.

Another lesson that I learned through my son is that you can feel the happiness of a person from within. Devin use to love to sing, "We are the salt of the earth. A bright light shining in a very dark world. While He's gone to prepare a place. We are the salt of the earth." He was a bright light shining, and there are plenty of people in this world who are the same. Devin woke up happy every day, and he taught me to do the same. I want to meet new people. I want to encourage them and tell them no matter how dark it gets, never stop shining. Trials and tribulations may come, but don't let that light go out. Even though the outcome may not always be in your favor, keep shining your way through. It is possible. I saw it done every single day.

The weekends were when Devin got a chance to tell me how his week was. He would want to spend the entire weekend following me around the house talking, playing, and spending quality time. He would explain a lot of things to me. For example, he would say, "Ma, you know when you put warm blankets on me, it makes me feel warm and snuggly inside, just like when you hug me."

That was an amazing revelation to me. I began to think about that, and I told him, "You are exactly right!" I could literally feel the warmth of his hugs on the inside. They were so soothing to my soul. That type of feeling should be displayed in all of your close relationships with family, friends, significant others, and spouses. If you don't feel that, you need to reevaluate that relationship, work to make it stronger, or maybe move on. I was given a gift that money can't buy. I know what it is and what it feels like to love unconditionally courtesy of my son!

Why do you want to get out of bed every morning?

Some days, I don't want to, but my reasons for getting out of bed are more important than staying in. I didn't fight and gain the strength that I have just to stay in bed and not share what I've gone through with someone who may be going through something similar. I wouldn't say that my life experiences are targeted toward a specific group. We all go through things, and even though every situation may not be the same, we can draw strength from the strong. No one can tell my story the way I can, so I have to get up and show up even on those days that are the hardest. I know that is what Devin would want. One of the many valuable lessons he taught me was to keep fighting when you think you don't have any fight left.

Why have you stayed at the same job for twenty years?

W hen I got this job twenty years ago, I needed more income. I was just trying to better myself so that I could provide for my children as a single mother with no long-term goals in mind. Twenty years later, the devil thought he had me stuck there. I'm thankful for where I've come from. The job paid some of the bills but not all.

In this moment, I want to encourage you, no matter what age you are, not to give up on your dreams. My slogan is "give your dreams life." I encourage you to pursue all your dreams! Do not settle for anything that doesn't allow you to reach your full potential. If you are wondering, it is possible to have multiple streams of income.

Five months after I got this job, Devin got sick. The job paid my bills when I was able to work but left me with nothing extra. When I was off with Devin, I had no money coming in. When he got better, I would return to work. I spent a lot of time trying to pay past-due bills, and I couldn't afford to take my children on vacations. I began to see what it felt like to live from paycheck to paycheck, but I thought that was okay, because that was all I saw growing up. I wanted more, but I began to see that I was trapped. I had children, and quitting my job to go back to school to get a degree was out of the question. I had little mouths to feed. I spent the next twenty years working in a place that was ripping me apart little by little and stunting my personal and financial growth. I couldn't reach my full potential working for someone else and fulfilling their dreams. As I continue to build my brand, I pray for the day that I am financially stable enough to walk away from corporate America.

Why am you writing another book?

I'm writing another book because I got a taste of what it's like to sow into myself for a change. As I stated, writing is therapy for me. It feels so good. It gives me the ability to explore my thoughts.

My kids who remain on earth are grown. They still need guidance but not as much supervised guidance as they did as babies. I have a lot of free time these days. I'm loving my new norm. Life is good.

I'm writing this book because there is a lot that goes along with my story. Not all of it is for the public to know, but there are parts that are encouraging that people need to know, and I want to share that.

Why do you want to manage a corporation?

I want to be a blessing to others. I want challenge myself and others to be different, to live out of the ordinary, and to live differently from what we are used to. I want more. Life is more than being contentedly unhappy where you are. I want to pay it forward in every way possible. I want to show you that you don't get where you want to be in life by sitting there. I want to empower, educate, and encourage everyone to be the best version of themselves. Live, love, and laugh with a purpose.

Why do you want to speak to millions?

I want to speak to millions because there are so many people who are going through the storm silently, some in ways similar to what I've gone through. Holding it in or trying to cope alone causes anxiety and depression. I understand that it's hard to trust people, because people will use what you tell them against you. I've been there. I thank God that I'm still standing. In reality, it takes only one person to relate to you and what you are going through. It makes a world of difference in your life. Just having someone who listens can change your life.

I have two friends who have helped me through this process, and I have talked to them every day. They are there for the anger, crying, and laughing. No matter what, they listen and give me feedback and advice. They have kept everything that I say between us, and I have done the same for them. They are both friends from childhood, and I love them dearly. I'm so grateful for their presence in my life. God sends people into your life for a season, and He definitely places people in your life for a lifetime.

By speaking, even if it's is a seasonal thing, I want to make a positive impact on people that they can carry for a lifetime. Maybe I can be an inspiration, but "seasonal" is far from what I am going to be. I will choose this path not just for building others—I'm helping and healing myself while I continue discovering who I am!

August 15, 2020

The time hops are crazy in this book, but who writes a book at one time?

I'm on the walking track, completing my fourth mile. I wanted to do three, but it feels so good out here. It's so peaceful! I'm in my element, in my zone: God, nature, and me. As the wind gently blows on my body, I have a sense of relaxation and peace. I'm so grateful for the countless times that God has allowed me to feel this. In the midst of whatever is going on in my life, God always finds a way to subtly say something to my spirit to let me know He's still here. I'm alone but not alone. I feel rejuvenated as my body is cleansed of toxins through the sweat that's coming out of my pores. The best feeling ever! When I'm walking and enjoying nature, my mind is clear, my spirit is free, and my body is soaking up all the benefits that come with these walks. When I'm out here on the track, internally and externally, I'm the best me I can be. These walks are more to me than just weight loss. They give me life.

At 3:22 on a Saturday morning, I'm awake. I have two hours left to sleep before I travel to Jackson to finish the final details before I launch my website. It's been a long and exhausting week but a life-changing one. When you need people the most, they will let you down. In the midst of all the letdown and disappointment, don't forget that you still have to get up and show up for yourself.

I've been taught that when you wake up in the middle of the night, that's God telling you to pray. Lord, I thank you for these quiet moments. Times like these allow my mind to rejuvenate itself. I get to channel in on myself without disturbances or distractions. Not only is there a sense of calmness and stillness inside the house, but that same calm and still demeanor is on the outside of the house as well. I'm grateful for the simple things that we take for granted.

August 26, 2020

I realize more than ever that weapons may form, but they will not prosper. I have the favor of God upon me! I am so thankful for the things that God works out in my favor. I am truly blessed. This year has been a year of revelation and restoration. I've had time to focus on myself, enabling me to realize who and what I need to pursue. I am walking out of this year so much stronger than I was before. I thought I was already strong, but each day, I realize that what I have been through has given me the strength and endurance to get to where I'm going.

I'm being restored in all areas of my life. The restoration is so powerful and so focused that I don't even realize it until I get to my next task. Thank you, Lord! I'm so grateful. I'm walking into the next phase of my life with confidence and assurance that I'm going to accomplish all of my dreams. Stay tuned for the next phase. Thank you for reading!

As the late John Lewis said, "I say to people today, you must be prepared if you believe in something. If you believe in something, you must go for it. As individuals, we may not live to see the end." Rest in peace, Congressman Lewis.

To those of you who got to the end of my book, I say preparation for the future is a must. Declutter your mind, and be prepared to live in the now! Life awaits, so go for it! Give your dreams life. I love you all!

Printed in the United States
By Bookmasters